MIRROR
OF
PERFECTION

CANTATA FOR SOPRANO & BARITONE SOLOISTS,
CHORUS AND ORCHESTRA
WITH TEXT BY ST FRANCIS OF ASSISI AND MUSIC BY

RICHARD BLACKFORD

VOCAL SCORE

NOVELLO

© 2002 Novello and Company Limited

Published in Great Britain by Novello Publishing Ltd.
(A division of Music Sales Limited)
Head office:
14/15 Berners Street,
London W1T 3LJ,
England
Tel +44 (0)20 7434 0066
Fax +44 (0)20 7287 6329

Sales and hire:
Music Sales Distribution Centre,
Newmarket Road,
Bury St. Edmunds,
Suffolk IP33 3YB,
England
Tel +44 (0)1284 702600
Fax +44 (0)1284 768301

www.chesternovello.com
e-mail: music@musicsales.co.uk

DURATION: c. 40 minutes

Mirror of Perfection is scored for Soprano and Baritone soli, SATB chorus,
horns, harp, percussion and strings

The orchestral material is available for hire from the publisher

Mirror of Perfection is recorded by Sony Classical (SK 60285)
with soprano Ying Huang, baritone Bo Skovhus,
Bournemouth Symphony Chorus and Bournemouth Sinfonietta,
conducted by the composer.

PART I
Canticle of the Creatures

Laudato sie, misignore,
Cum tucte le tue Creature,
Spetialmente messor lo frate sole,
Lo qual è iorno et allumini noi per poi.
Et ellu è bellu e radiante
Cum grande splendore
Da te, Altissimo, porta significatione.

Laudato sie, misignore,
Per sora luna e le stelle,
In celu l'ài formate clarite et pretiose et belle.

Laudato sie, misignore, per frate vento
Et per aere et nubilo et sereno
Et onne tempo,
Per lo quale a le tue creature
Dai sustentamento.

Laudato sie, misignore, per sor' acqua,
La quale è multo utile et humile
Et pretiosa et casta.

Laudato sie, misignore, per frate focu,
Per lo quale ennallumini la nocte.
Ed ello è bello et iocundo
Et robustoso et forte.

Laudato sie, misignore,
Per sora nostra matre terra,
La quale ne sustenta et governa
Et produce diversi fructi
Con coloriti flori et herba.

Altissimo, omnipotente bonsignore
Tue so' le laude, la gloria et l'honore,
Et onne benedictione.

All praise be yours, my Lord,
For all your creatures,
Specially for Brother Sun,
Who brings the day and the light to us.
He is beautiful and radiant
In all his splendour
To you, Most High, he bears likeness.

All praise be yours, my Lord,
For Sister Moon and Stars,
You made them bright, precious and fair in heaven.

All praise be yours, my Lord,
For Brothers Wind and Air, fair and stormy
All the weather's moods,
For the sustenance
Of all your creatures.

All praise be yours, my Lord, for Sister Water,
So useful, humble,
Precious and pure.

All praise be yours, my Lord, for Brother Fire,
Through whom you brighten the night.
He is beautiful and jocund,
Full of power and strength.

All praise be yours, my Lord,
For our Sister Mother Earth,
Who sustains and governs us
And produces various fruits
With coloured flowers and herbs.

Most high, all powerful, Lord of Goodness,
All Praise is yours, all glory and honour
And all blessing.

PART II
Canticle of Love – Part One

Amor di caritate,
Perchè m'hai si ferito?
Lo cor tutt'ho partito,
Ed arde per amore.
Arde ed incende, e nullo trova loco:
Non può fuggire, però ch'è ligato:
Sì si consuma, come cera a foco;

Love of loves,
Why have you so wounded me?
My heart, torn from its dwelling
Is consumed with love.
It is on fire, it burns, it finds no resting place:
It cannot escape, because it is chained:
It is consumed, like wax in the fire.

Vivendo muor, languisce stemperato:
E domanda poter fuggire un poco,
Ed in fornace trovasi locato,
Oimè do' son menato
A si forte languire?
Vivendo si è morire:
Tanto monta l'ardore.

Dying, it lives, its languor is sweet:
It prays for power to escape,
And finds itself a furnace,
Alas where will I be lead
By this terrible faintness?
It is death to live like this:
Such is the stifling heat of this fire.

PART III
Canticle of the Furnace

In foco l'Amor mi mise:
In foco l'Amor mi mise:
Divisemi lo core,
E 'l corpo cadè in terra.
Quel quadrel dell'amore,
Che balestra disserra,
Percosse con ardore,
Di pace fece guerra.
Moromi di dolciore.

Love has cast me in a furnace:
Love has cast me in a furnace:
He has pierced my heart,
And my body has fallen to the ground
The arrows fired
From his bow of love,
Have struck me,
He has turned peace into war.
I am dying of sweetness.

In foco l'Amor mi mise:
Le sorti, che mandava,
Eran pietre piombate,
Che ciascuna gravava
Mille libre pesate:
Si spesse le gittava,
Non le'arei numerate;
Nulla mai ne fallava.

Love has cast me in a furnace:
The darts which he threw
Were lead-covered stones,
Each one weighing
Thousands of pounds:
They rained on me, like thick hail;
I was unable to count them;
Not one missed its mark.

[In foco l'Amor mi mise:]
Non mai arebbe fallato;
Si ben trarle sapeva.
In terra ero io sternato,
Aitar non mi poteva;
Tutto era fracassato:
Niente più mi senteva,
Com' uom ch'era passato.

Love has cast me in a furnace:
He never missed me once;
Such was his good aim.
I was lying on the ground,
My limbs could not assist me;
My body was broken;
I had no more feeling,
Than a dead man.

In foco l'Amor mi mise:
Passato, non per morte,
Ma di gioia adescato:
Poi rivissi sì forte
Dentro dal cor fermato,
Che seguii quelle scorte,
Che m'aveano guidato
Nella superna Corte.

Love has cast me in a furnace:
Not on account of death,
But because of joy:
After my body recovered
I became so strong,
That I could follow the guides,
Who conducted me
To the gates of heaven.

PART IV
Canticle of Love – Part Two

Chè cielo e terra grida, e sempre clama	*Heaven and earth and all creation cry out to me*
E tutte cose, che io sì debbia amare.	*That I must love.*
Ciascuna dice: con tutto core ama	*Everything tells me: with all your heart*
L'amor, ch'ha'fatto briga d'abbracciare;	*Love the love that loves you;*
Chè quell'amore, per ciò che t'abbrama	*Love the love which desires you*
Tutti noi ha fatti per a se tirare.	*Which has created you to draw you*
Veggo tanto abbondare	*Wholly to itself*
Bontade e cortesìa	*Therefore I desire never to stop drawing*
Da quella luce pia,	*On this holy light*
Che si spande di fore.	*And this ineffable goodness.*
Bellezza antiqua e nuova,	*O goodness, old and always new,*
[Da poi] che t'ho trovata;	*Which I have found*
O luce smisurata	*O immense Light*
Di si dolce spendore!	*Whose splendour is so sweet!*

PART V
Canticle of the Birds

Mes frères, les petits oiseaux,	*My Brothers, the birds,*
Vous devez louer votre Créateur	*You should praise your Creator*
Et l'aimer toujours.	*And always love him.*
Car il vous a donné	*For he has given you*
Des plumes pour vous couvrir,	*Feathers to cover you,*
Des ailes pour voler,	*Wings with which to fly,*
Et tout ce qui vous avez.	*And everything you need.*
Il vous a fait nobles	*He has made you noble*
Entre tous les ouvrages de ses mains,	*Among all his works,*
Il vous a choisi une demeure	*He has chosen for you a dwelling*
Dans la pure région de l'air.	*In the pure region of air.*
Et sans que vous ayez besoin de semer	*And without your needing to sow*
Ni moissoner,	*Nor reap,*
Sans vous laisser aucune sollicitude,	*You are delivered from all care*
Il vous nourrit et vous gouverne.	*He sustains and governs you.*
Mes frères, les petits oiseaux,	*My Brothers, the birds,*
Vous devez louer votre Créateur	*You should praise your Creator*
Et l'aimer toujours.	*And always love him.*

PART VI
Canticle of Love – Part Three

Amore, Amore, che sì m'hai ferito.	*Love, Love, who has so wounded me.*
Altro, che amore, non posso gridare.	*I can only utter one cry, Love.*
Amore, Amore, teco sono unito,	*Love, Love, I am united to you,*
Altro non posso che te abbracciare	*I can only embrace you.*
Amore, Amor, si forte m'hai rapito,	*Love, Love who has so ravished me,*
Lo core sempre spando per amare.	*My heart grows weaker with love.*
Per te vo'spasimare:	*I am absorbed in you:*
Amor, ch'io teco sia:	*Love, let me abide with you:*
Amor, per cortesìa	*Love, in your goodness*
Fammi morir d'Amore.	*Let me die of love.*
Amore, Amore grida tutto'l mondo:	*Love, Love, it is the cry of the whole world:*
Amore, Amore ogni cosa clama:	*Love, Love, it is the cry of everything:*
Amore, Amore tanto se'profondo,	*Love, Love, such is your depth,*
Chi più t'abbraccia sempre più t'abbrama.	*The more embraced, the more desired.*
Amore, Amor, tu sei cerchio rotondo;	*Love, Love, you are the circle around my heart;*
Con tutto 'l cor, chi c'entra, sempre t'ama;	*He who possesses you, loves you forever;*
Chè tu se'strame e trama:	*You are my food and my clothing:*
Chi t'ama di vestire	*He who loves you*
Dai si dolce sentire,	*Is happy to feel your sweetness,*
Che sempre grida Amor.	*To forever cry, Love.*
Amore, Amor tanto penar mi fai.	*Love, Love, you make me suffer so.*
Amore, Amore nol posso patire:	*Love, Love, I cannot bear it.*
Amore, Amore tanto mi tì dai,	*Love, Love, you give me so much,*
Amore, Amore, ben credo morire:	*Love, Love, I think I will die:*
Amore, Amore, tanto preso m'hai,	*Love, Love, you have so much dominion over me,*
Amore, Amore, fammi in te transire:	*Love, Love, transform me into yourself:*
Amor dolce languire	*Love, sweet languor*
Amor mio desioso	*Love my desire*
Amor mio dilettoso	*Love my delight*
Annegami in Amore.	*Bind me with love.*
Amore, Amore, lo cor sì mi si spezza,	*Love, Love, my heart is broken*
Amore, Amore, tal sento ferita:	*Love, Love, my heart is wounded:*
Amore, Amor, trammi alla tua bellezza,	*Love, Love, draw me towards your beauty,*
Amore, Amor, per te sono rapita:	*Love, Love, I am ravished by you:*
Amore, Amor vivere disprezza,	*Love, Love, disdaining life*
Amore, Amore, l'alma teco unita.	*Love, Love my soul is united with you*
Amor, tu sei mia vita:	*Love, you are my life:*
Già non si può partire,	*Do not forsake me,*
Perchè la fai languire	*For you have made me faint*
Tanto struggendo, Amore.	*All-embracing Love.*

PART VII
Canticle of Peace

Beati quelli kel sosteranno in pace,	*Blessed are the peacemakers,*
Ka da te, Altissimo, sirano incoronati.	*By you, Most High, they will be crowned.*

(translated by Richard Blackford)

for Lila

Mirror of Perfection

Words by St Francis of Assisi

Music by Richard Blackford

Part 1
Canticle of the Creatures

2

(for rehearsal only until bar 21)

Animando

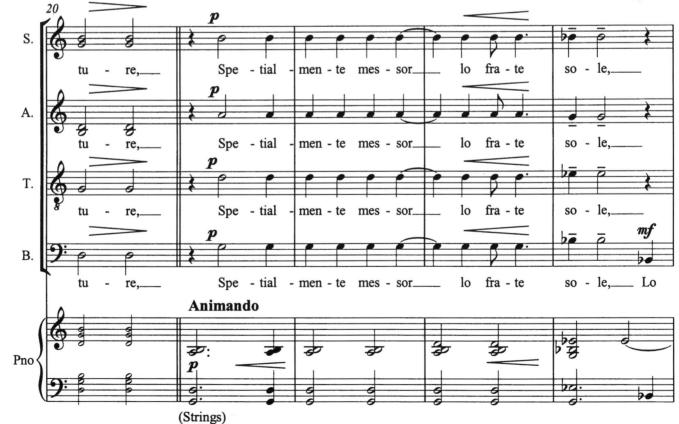

(Strings)

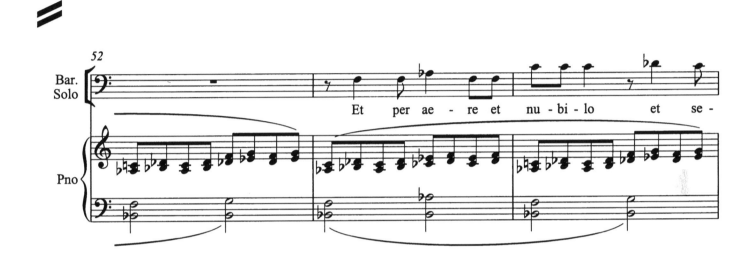

8

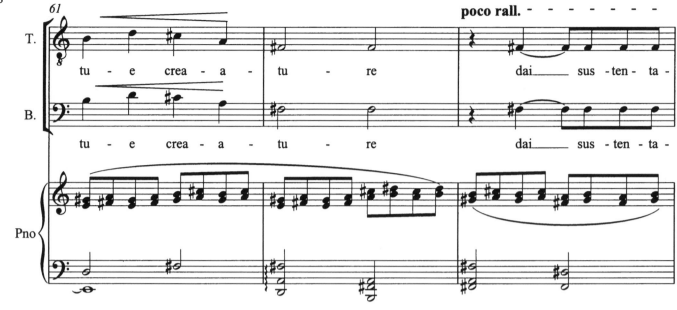

tu - e cre - a - tu - re dai___ sus - ten - ta -

tu - e cre - a - tu - re dai___ sus - ten - ta -

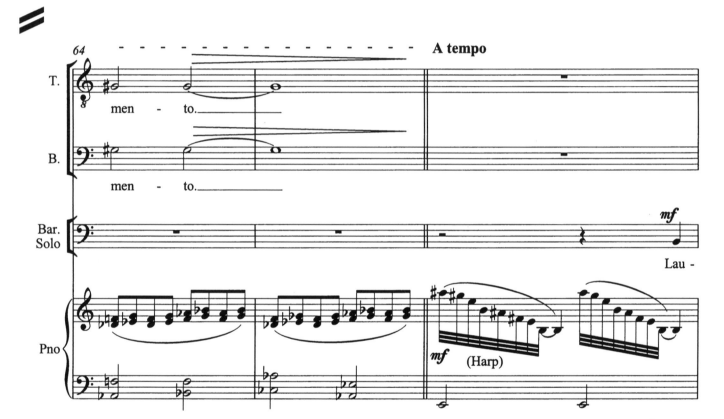

men - to.___

men - to.___

Lau -

(Harp)

da - to sie, mi - si - gno - re,___

10

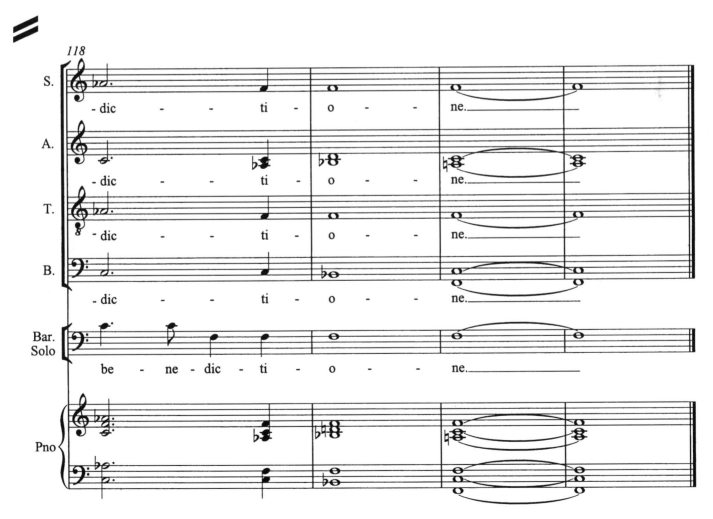

Part II
Canticle of Love I

A - mor di ca - ri - ta - te, Per - chè

— m'hai si fe - ri - to? Lo cor tutt' ho par - ti - to, Ed

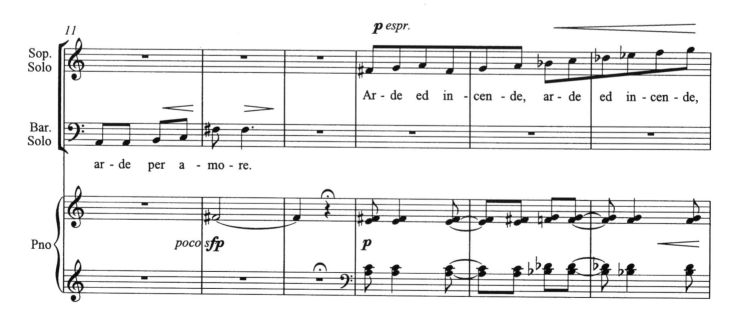

Ar - de ed in - cen - de, ar - de ed in - cen - de,

ar - de per a - mo - re.

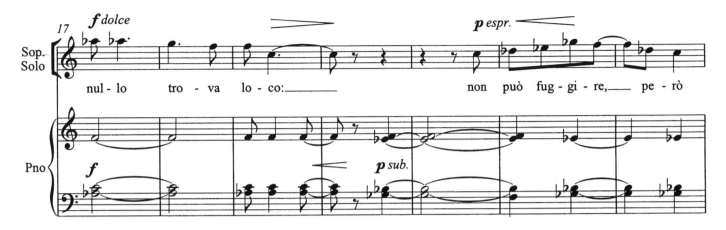

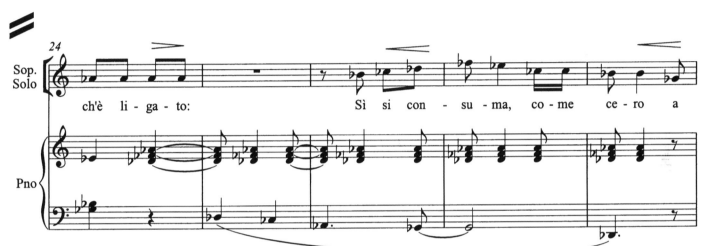

-sce stem-pe - - ra - - to e do-man-da po-ter fug - gi - re un

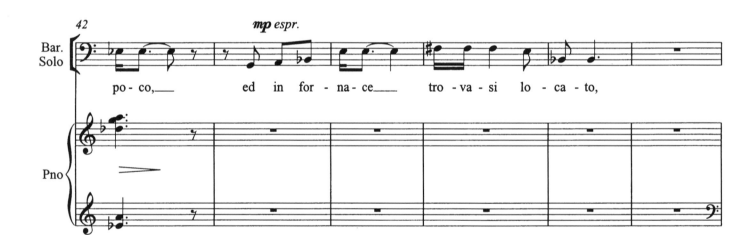

po - co,___ ed in for - na - ce___ tro-va-si lo-ca-to,

Oi - mè do' son me - na - to a sì for - te lan-gui-re? Vi-

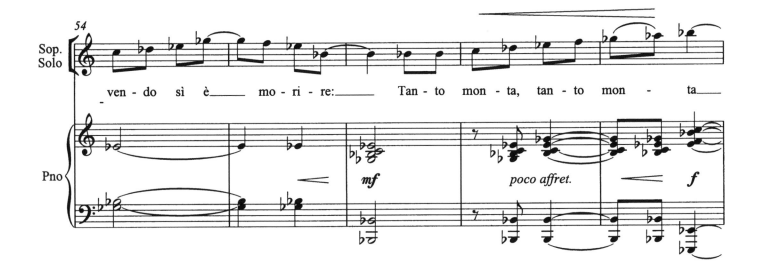

ven-do sì è____ mo-ri-re:____ Tan-to mon-ta, tan-to mon- ta____

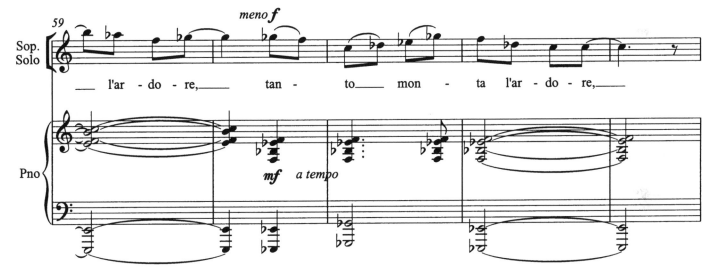

__l'ar-do-re,____ tan- to____ mon- ta l'ar-do-re,____

l'ar - do - re._____

Part III
Canticle of the Furnace

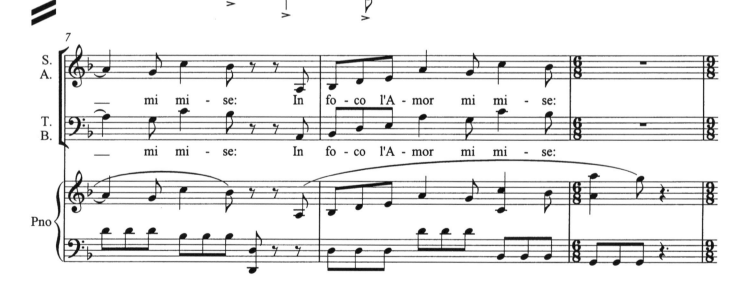

Quel qua - drel ___ dell' a - mo - re, Che ba-les-tra dis-ser - ra, Per cos - se

Per cos - se

con ar - do - re, di pa - ce fe - ce guer - ra. Mo - ro - mi, mo - ro - mi,

con ar - do - re, di pa - ce fe - ce guer - ra. Mo - ro - mi, mo - ro - mi,

mo - ro - mi di dol - cio - re.

mo - ro - mi di dol - cio - re.

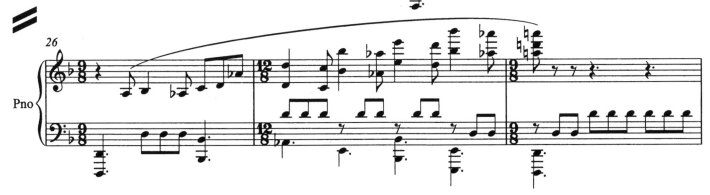

22

In fo-co l'A-mor____ mi mi - se: In fo-co l'A-mor mi mi - se:

In fo-co l'A-mor____ mi mi - se: In fo-co l'A-mor mi mi - se:

Le sor - ti, che man - da - va, E ran pie - tre piom-ba-te,

Che cia - scu - na gra - va - va Mil - le

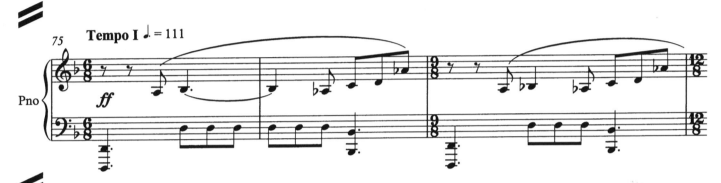

26

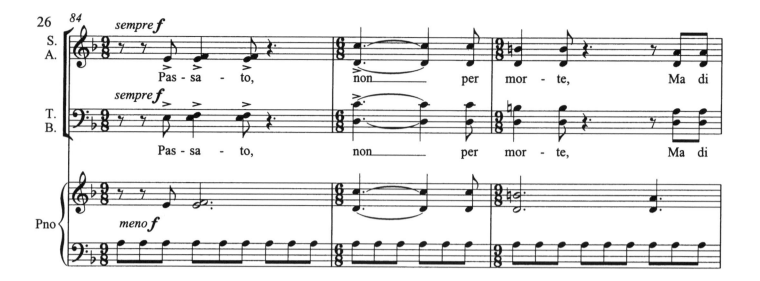

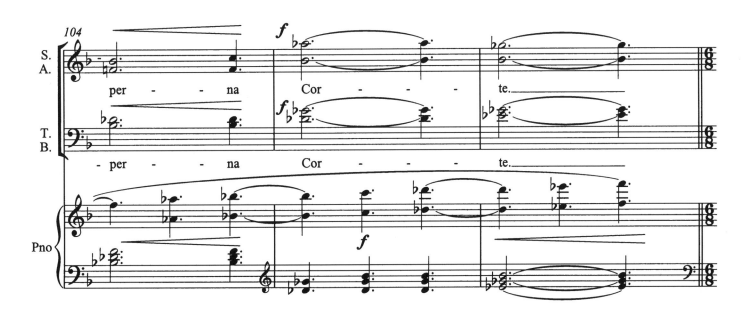

Tempo I

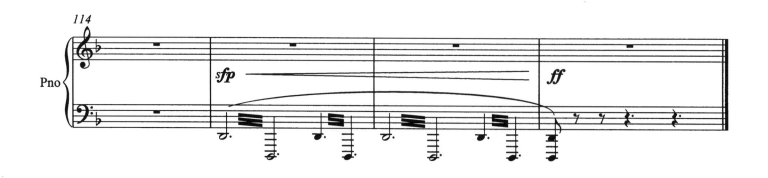

Part IV
Canticle of Love II

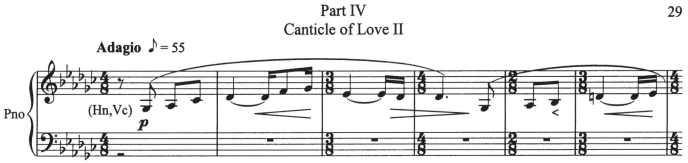

Chè cie - lo e ter - ra gri - da e sem - pre cla - ma,

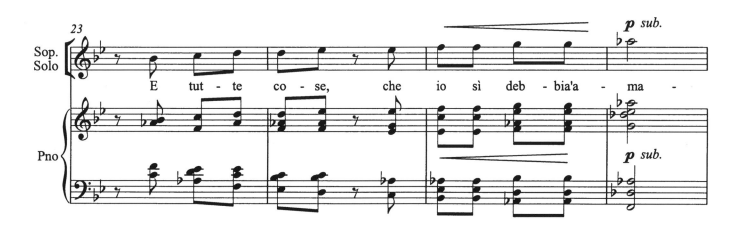

E tut - te co - se, che io sì deb - bia'a - ma -

Poco più mosso

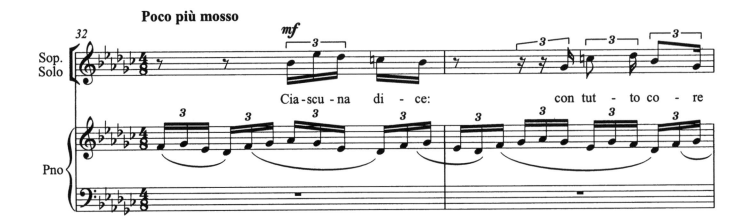

Cia - scu - na di - ce: con tut - to co - re

a - ma L'a - mor_____ ch'ha fat - to bri - ga_____ d'ab - brac - cia - re;

Chè quel - l'a - mo - re, per

ciò che t'ab - bra - ma Tut - ti noi___ ha fat - ti per a se - ti-

Maestoso ♪ = 72

ff joyfully

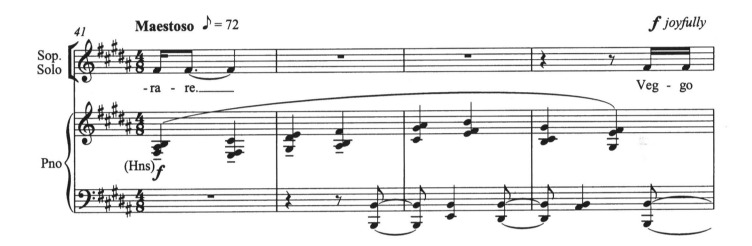

-ra - re.___ Veg - go

(Hns) *f*

tan - to___ ab - bon - da - re___ Bon ta - de e cor - te - sì - a___

Da quel - la lu - ce pi - a,___ Che si span - de___ di fo - re.___

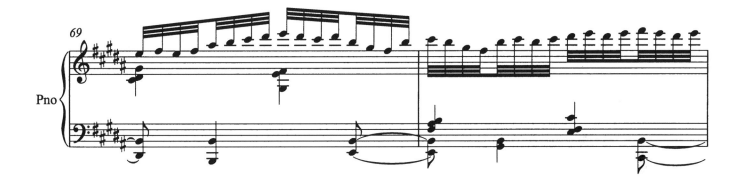

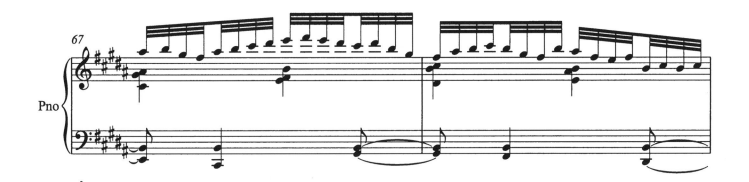

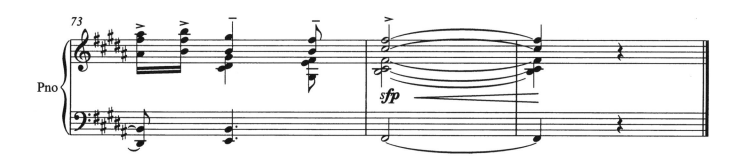

Part V
Canticle of the Birds

Mes frères,_____ les pe - tits oi -

seaux,_____ Vous de - vez lou - er_____ vòtre Cré__ a -

teur_____ Et l'ai - mer,_____ l'ai - mer tou -

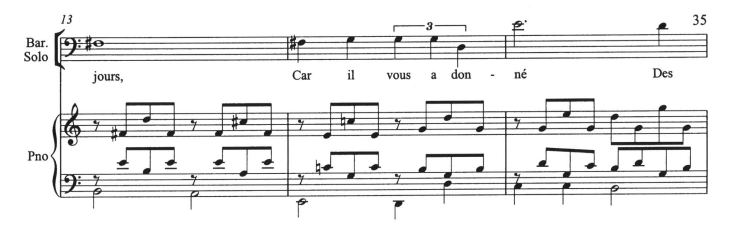

36

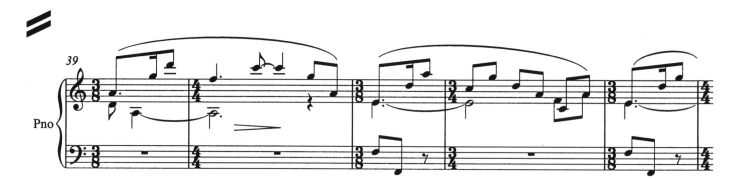

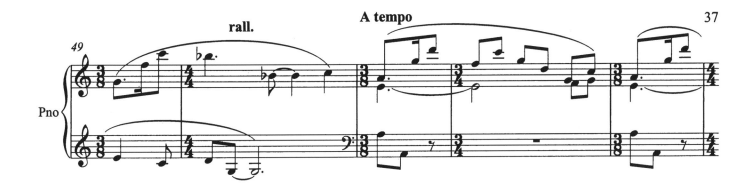

rall. . . . . A tempo

S
Mes frères ___ les pe-tits oi - seaux,

Bar. Solo

Pno

S
___ vous de-vez lou - er ___ vôtre Cré ___ a -teur

Bar. Solo

Pno

rall. Tempo I

Bar. Solo
Il vous a choi - si ___ u - ne de - meure ___

Pno

Bar. Solo
___ Dans la pu - re ré - gi - on de

Pno

✻ Where children's voices are incoporated in the choir, this movement is ideally suited to trebles alone (ad libitum).

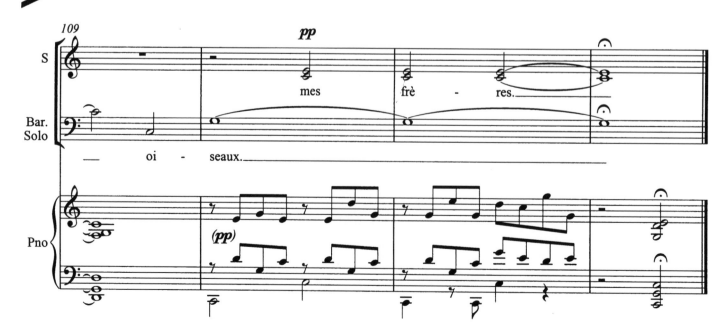

Part VI
Canticle of Love III

48

Part VII
Canticle of Peace

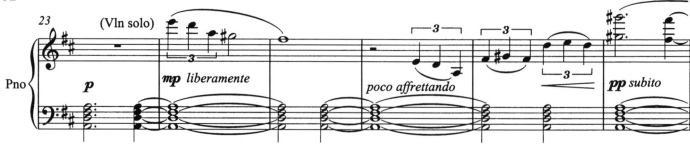

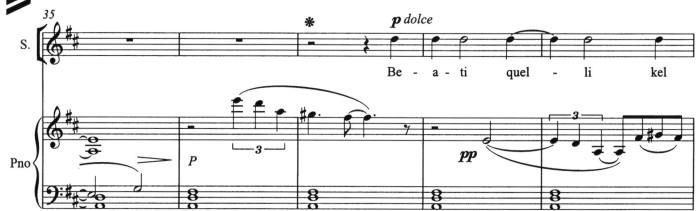

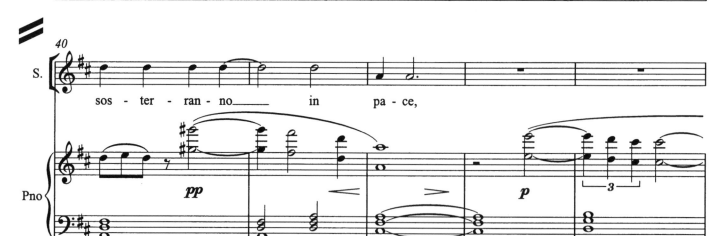

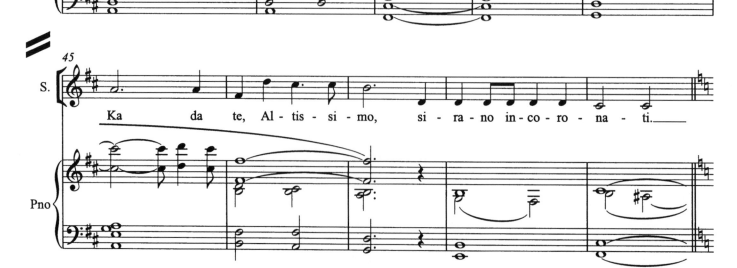

111111111111